Guidebook for Working with Small Independent Publishers

by Terry Persun

Hoai,

Learning the rules is only the first step. Breaking them is the fun part.

Guidebook for Working with Small Independent Publishers

Contents:

Chapter 1: Make a Decision

There are more ways to get published today than there ever have been. The easiest method, if you have the money and time, is to self publish your book. If you choose to go this way in print, there are plenty of short run (typically between 250 and 2500 copies) printers, design houses, and publishers who will help you through the process, some of which use POD (print on demand) technology and some that do not. If you choose to go the self-publishing route as an e-book (an electronic book rather than a printed book), there are an equal number of places to go for help. Or you can upload your work to a website (your own?) or produce a PDF and email it around the world. A PDF (Portable Document Format) is a standard used to reduce the file size of brochures, magazines, books, etc. so that they are easily emailed.

7

But if you're looking to get your book published through traditional methods where you find an editor (whether through an agent or not) who loves your writing and will help you develop it, will perform editing functions, and works for a publishing company that will print the book, then there are some things you need to know.

For the purposes of this book, I'm going to suggest two categories of publishers: large publishers and small presses. Generally, a large publisher is one that prints hundreds of titles a year, in runs of 5000 copies or greater, and offers an advance against royalties for the books they buy. Small publishers (including University presses) print fewer than 30 books a year, often in runs of less than 2500 copies, and do not offer an advance against royalties. Another key difference between the two is that large publishing houses usually don't read manuscripts unless they are handled by an agent. There are books about how to get an agent out there and if that is the way you want to go, I suggest you look there first. If, on the other hand, you feel that your work doesn't lend itself to the mass market needs of the large publishing houses, then there are small presses and university presses that might be the way to go. In this book the terms small press, small publisher, and university press will be used interchangeably.

Writers are typically readers. Find and read books

similar to the type you write. Look up the publisher to see if they qualify as a large or small press. Then do some research to find other publishers who acquire similar books. You'll notice that there are often large and small publishers acquiring books similar to those you write. Even if you're writing genre fiction that fits into a category in the bookstore like mystery, romance, or fantasy, you'll find that there are large and small presses to work with. If you ultimately choose to go after a larger publisher, getting an agent might be your first step.

Some of you are reading this book because you've tried the agent route and that didn't work for you. Either you couldn't get an agent, or the agent you did get couldn't sell your book. It's been a few years and you'd like to see something happen with the book you've written. Perhaps you came to this book because you've had a book or two published by a larger publisher, but the books didn't sell through and now publishers aren't interested in working with you for your new book. There are a lot of authors, considered mid-list authors, or those who have not sold enough books to maintain the interest of a large publisher. The small press provides a way to get published where selling a few thousand books makes you one their star performers.

An editor of a small publishing house once told me this: "If a small publisher doesn't sell very many copies of your book, it's viewed as the publisher's fault. But, if a large publisher doesn't sell enough copies of your books, it's viewed as your book's fault." This simple statement may be reason enough to start out with a small publisher if you're a beginning writer.

Ultimately, this book is more about where to focus your energy. Do a little homework and make an informed decision where to go with your book. If you believe that working with a small press is right for you, then commit to it. Research the presses (through writer's directories), read books published by small presses (available through most bookstores and/or amazon.com), and go to conferences and workshops where small press editors or publishers are present (visit shawguides.com for a list of these).

If you've read this far, you are probably considering working with small presses. The good news is that while there are only a few (five conglomerates (multinational publishing corporations) and maybe another five large independents (non-corporate publishers that still meet the criteria of a large publisher as mentioned above)) major publishers in the U.S. today, there are literally thousands of small publishers to choose from. Plus, small presses cover all genres of novels and literally every subject matter you can imagine. In fact, the narrowest niche books – academic evaluations of literary figures, specific titles on small Indian tribes, or analytical books on particular plant species – are only being published by small or university presses these days.

The even better news is that these publishers are not only open to new authors, they welcome them and are often willing to work with an author they like for years to come. Many small publishers will help you develop your art and will be right beside you all the way. In fact this is so true that there are thousands of authors who now publish with large houses because they started out with a dedicated editor and publisher from a small house that produced a short run of each title.

Most small presses do not pay an advance towards royalties, which means that most agents won't reach out to a small press for their clients precisely because there is no advance involved. I'm talking about very small publishers, and micro publishers, houses that put out up to ten titles a year (sometimes more, but usually fewer), houses that may also run a magazine or print chapbooks.

I'm not suggesting that working with a small press is better or worse than working with a large publisher. I have no axe to grind with agents or publishers. The truth is, I have an agent for books that I believe are geared toward a larger audience and could sell better through a large publisher, but I also write books that are not suited to a large publisher's needs. I write poetry that I always send out to a small press.

If you write novels, your decision may not be so easy. Since I've written novels, too, I know that the first thought you have is that the book could (or should) sell to a large audience. But novels, like the characters in them, appear to have legs of their own. Even the publishers of novels will tell you that they have no idea what the public will sink their teeth into next. They don't know what the next fly-off-the-shelf novel will be. They can hope, they can guess, but they don't know. We'll talk about novels more in later chapters. So don't be discouraged. There is a place for everything. Which reminds me of another statement I read once. It was written about publishing poetry in small, independent magazines, and was before the internet came along. But it's still a relevant statement, and I believe fits the mood here. To paraphrase: "If you haven't been published in the small press yet, it's most likely because you haven't spent enough money on postage." Now, with Internet submissions, you don't even have to spend money on postage.

Chapter 2: The Good News

I like to start with the good news first. And there are plenty of good reasons why publishing with a small press creates a positive experience. First and foremost small presses are willing to take risks. Small publishers typically start up because they believe that large publishers focus too much on money and not enough on art. Small publishers are looking for something different than the stock best seller or the standard romance. It's not that these publishers don't want to make money, they do, but they want to do it through discovering something new as opposed to publishing the standard fare. These publishers are looking for the next important and talented writer, the one who breaks the rules but still writes a great novel. A similar statement can be said about non-fiction as well. Small presses are not afraid to publish controversial material, or material that has a narrow reader segment.

Some small presses start out publishing newsletters or magazines or websites on a certain subject, like fly tying, wood duck carving, or black women poets, and find that its audience grows to a high enough number that it begins to produce books to feed the market. Other publishers start up to fill out a narrow niche market that they feel isn't fully covered. These publishers are typically passionate about the subject matter, like model trains, baseball, or doll making. In this case, a publisher may produce a book on N size model trains, signed baseball collections, or only rag dolls.

Small publishers seldom care if you switch subjects or genres as long as it's something they're interested in publishing. For example, if you write a fantasy and then want to write a mystery, small publishers are more likely to go along with the switch. Where large publishers like an author to stick with what they've written before and what the publisher knows it can sell, small publishers are not as concerned about it. This is why there are mainstream authors who also publish with small presses.

Small press publishers are more likely to follow you than to guide you, which is the epitome of taking risks. This doesn't mean that they won't suggest ideas, it only means that the publisher won't tend to drop you if you try something different.

As I've mentioned briefly, small publishers are producing books in every niche imaginable, and because of this they are also working in a variety of sizes and formats to fit the particular subject and/or readership: standard mass market paperback, trade paperback, hardback, four color oversize hardback or paperback, and many other formats – and these are just the print ones. Small press publishers in poetry are particularly known for their explorations: of using different types or colors of paper, producing booklets in odd sizes or shapes, and incorporation unique binding techniques. These publishers are artists in their own right, and may work with old printing machines or hand presses. They may use woodblock prints as internal artwork, or produce a unique three-dimensional cover. They want the entire experience to be artistic, from the writing of the work, to the layout, the materials, and the production. These publishers produce beautiful books in every way, and worth every penny that is paid for them.

A key benefit for some writers who choose to work with small presses is time to market. Because the editor who read and liked your book is often the publisher, and may be the person to lay the book out and interface with the printer and wholesaler, time to market can be much shorter than the 12 to 24 months you'd expect to get from larger publishers. Small publishers only accept as many books as they can handle, and work diligently to get through the process. It's a project that they are excited and passionate about. It's not just a job. They want to see the book in its final form as much as you do, so they'll work on it until it's complete.

One of the things I like best about working with a small publisher is that they are open to author input throughout the publishing process. They want you to be as proud of the book as they are. They think of you as a partner, not just an author. They'll respect your ideas and thoughts and they'll try their best to produce the book well.

We've all gone online or to a bookstore (my preference) and been told that a book is out of print. The reason is typically because the particular book sold so few copies a month that it wasn't worth the money to warehouse it. So, the books are either remaindered or thrown away. Although many small presses will only print a limited number of books (unless they offer POD services too), they will keep your book for years. As long as copies are available, they'll sell them rather than discount them to make room for another, better selling book. Small presses hold large backlists, which eventually become the backbone of their sales efforts. As new books by the same author come out, the backlist sells better. It's part of their strategy, and it helps them stay profitable. Because of minimal out of pocket costs and low press runs, they can afford to do this.

Remember, there are thousands of small presses to

choose from. This means that your book isn't dead in the water after being rejected by the first ten publishers, or the first hundred. There are plenty more to choose from and more starting up every day. This is especially true for fiction. According to the "International Directory of Little Magazines and Small Publishers" there are literally hundreds of small presses starting up each year. Fiction and poetry are considered art forms, and an editor who chooses to publish your novel or poetry collection often looks at it that way. And each small press editor or publisher is different, and is looking for something different in the books they choose. To echo where I ended in chapter one, if you're not published you haven't tried submitting to enough presses yet. Rest assured that there's one out there for you. But before you take the leap, there are a few drawbacks to consider.

Chapter 3: The Not So Good News

The drawbacks of working with small presses often extend from the worse side of the benefits mentioned in the previous chapter. I know because I've been a part of both sides. It's a learning process.

I've mentioned that the small press publisher/editor is passionate about the books he or she produces. For that reason he may not be in it for the money. But that might be the primary reason you're writing. When money isn't the focus of the publisher, risk increases for the author. I said that the small press publishers would take risks, and this is the negative result of that character trait. Most authors I know want to gain monetarily from their work – not all, by the way. A publisher that makes a book available then forgets about it when the next project comes up hasn't given the book a chance to find its paying audience. The poetry booklet publisher mentioned in the last chapter may be the model for this type of publisher. With unique bindings and specially made papers, such a press might produce ten truly original pieces of art, sell them to a few collectors, and then move on to the next project. Unless you have a second book that's coming out on the tail of the first, your book project continues to get less and less attention as time goes on.

Small publishers finish a project and then become entrenched in the next project immediately. It's a good idea to talk with the publisher to see where their interests or talents lie. Sometimes you can get a hint by looking at their website's "about" section. If they talk exclusively about their selection process, they may not be focused enough on sales. Hopefully, their site discusses what types of books they are looking for and how they plan to get them out to the public. If you're an author who wants to continue to write and publish, you need to reach an audience. It doesn't have to be a large audience, but a loyal one.

Once again, because small presses are often into the next project pretty quickly, communication with them can begin to slow down. In fact, for presses whose publisher has a regular nine-to-five job, getting back to an author is a nights and weekends affair anyway. I produced a small press poetry magazine, Goblets, for several years. I spent a few evenings, most lunch hours, and every weekend culling through poetry submissions. I had a full time job and was going to college part time. I loved publishing the magazine, and even produced several chapbooks, but burned out quickly. It was almost impossible for me to write notes to poets, make phone calls, or even market the magazine outside of a few directories. It's a tough job, but I loved it while it lasted.

This leads to the next drawback on my list: the publisher closes the press down. This can happen because the person finds that running a small press isn't as much fun as they thought, because it's so overwhelming that they burn out quickly, because their life changes (they get married, divorced, lose their job), or simply because they run out of money. Over the years, I've communicated with several small start-up publishers who gained an inheritance after a close relative died and started to publish books – a lifelong dream. When the inheritance was gone, the press closed its doors. They were passionate people, but didn't know how to run a business. Over half of the small presses that start in a given year go out of business in less than three years.

Small publishers plan on small press runs. So I recommend that authors pre-sell their books to friends and relatives very early in the process. Early sales may influence the total number of books published. Most small publishers do not reprint once a book project is completed. If they normally print 2500 copies of a novel, for instance, the novel becomes out of print when those copies are gone. If you can pre-sell 700 copies, the publisher may choose to print 3500, which works in your favor for two reasons: first you have more books available to sell, and second your book has nearly paid for itself right away. (Break even for small runs can range from thirty to fifty percent of the run depending on the price points used.)

One of the worst things about small publishers in my mind is that you usually only have one editor working with you (also mentioned as a benefit in the previous chapter). There are no proofreaders after the book is gone through by the editor. If you're lucky, you get a galley to check out before it goes to press. This means that more mistakes can pass through. These editors are not less talented or less educated; they're more strung out, busier with life, and physically tired.

As mentioned at the beginning of this chapter, this is another area where you can help. My suggestion is to have several writer friends (who are honest with you) go through your manuscript before sending it out. Then each section that you adjust for your editor you also pass through your own readers to make sure that your adjustments didn't create new problems. This gives you a better chance of sending clean copy to your editor. If your publisher provides a galley for a final check, have several readers go through it. This is the number one problem with self-published books, there weren't enough good readers and the manuscript is a mess grammatically, thematically, or organizationally. For authors who wish to self publish, this is even more important. Hire an editor or two!

Small presses do not always produce professional-looking covers. I have a few friends who claim they can tell a book was done by a small press or was self-published based strictly on the cover art and layout. Of course this is not true all the time. Many small publishers do employ art directors, whether paid or not. I've actually seen some of the best covers coming out of the small presses. As mentioned in the good news section, publishers who see the entire book process and all its parts as an art form unto itself often spend as much time or more on the cover as on the written words inside. Plus, once again, you can have an affect on this by hiring your own cover designer or artist. Most of the small presses I've worked with over the years have been more than happy to have me hire someone to do the cover. In a few cases the publisher would use the same artist for other titles as well. My artist friend was happy for the introduction.

Limited resources for small presses, whether editorially or graphically, means that there is little to no recourse if a problem is found after the project is completed. Bad cover design, grammatical mistakes, poor binding quality — too late. As a concerned author it's necessary that you are available and helpful throughout the production process. Don't be a pest, but be diligent. My recommendation is to buy several of the books produced by the small publisher as soon as your project is accepted (or before if possible). Read the books. Evaluate the editing, the design, the physical production. If the publisher is really good at any one part of the process, it'll stand out. That's the part that you need to be concerned with the least.

Small publishers are not always the best marketers. It may be that small press publishers are artists in their own right, and that the business side of things is more difficult for them. I tend to believe it's because marketing is labor intensive, not because they don't know how to do the job, or have little talent in that area. Setting up readings takes time, mailing and following up on review copies takes time, and making sure books are available at every event the author might wish to attend takes time. Yes, it takes money too, but mostly it's the time concerned that gets in the way of the next project. Not to belabor the point, but when the publisher also has a full time job, some of the above acts can't get completed during the day and are literally impossible to perform after work hours.

It's up to the author to create a marketing plan that they can afford and have the time to execute. Think of it as a part time job. This will be one way to turn a negative into a positive. And marketing is the one thing that an author can and must handle if they are to help their small press sell their books.

The last item, distribution, used to be difficult for most small presses. For niche publishers their audiences would have been developed before the first book was produced, but for general fiction publishers finding your readers can be like a treasure hunt, and distribution can only help.

Bookstores buy books through wholesalers like Ingram and Baker & Taylor. They don't like to buy books through individual catalogs from hundreds of small publishers. That would be a lot of work, which would take time from running their bookstore.

Before working with a small press, research how they distribute their books. A company like Small Press Distribution produces a catalog with hundreds of small publishers represented and has made it much easier for a bookstore to order small press titles. Even the larger wholesalers are open to small presses if the sales are high enough and if the press offers enough titles. Your active participation in selling your title can help your small publisher sell other books as well. Be a good partner and do what you can to help sell and you'll find that your publisher will stay alive longer and become a stronger partner for you.

Now, with chapter four we get into more detail.

Chapter 4: How to Contact Small Publishers

I've established that small presses operate differently than large publishers. And one of the most obvious differences comes in the way you make first contact. Small publishers have fewer of what I like to call "filters or roadblocks." To begin with, you don't need to go through an agent. In a business where getting from concept to reader is a slow process to begin with, removing steps along the way can mean a lot. For example, if the typical method is to query an agent, and then sign on with an agent who then queries an editor who has to clear the project through other editors and often through marketing before you are even offered a contract, then removing the need for an agent just saved you months or perhaps years of time.

Small press publishers are everywhere. There could

25

be a person running a small press working at the same company where you work. Your neighbor might be a small press publisher. You never know, so stay on the lookout.

Like most other businesses – and I consider writing as much as a business as an art – face-to-face contact often works best in selling yourself and your work. So my first recommendation is to go where small press and university press publishers go. Conferences like the AWP (Associated Writing Programs) will have a lot of publishers and editors present. These events are held for several days and offer workshops on writing, editing, and publishing. If you've already been published by any of the magazines or publishers who show up at these conferences, introduce yourself. Get to know them better. Get to know who they know.

There are literally thousands of writers' conferences and book fairs and poetry slams and on and on that are being hosted and attended by hundreds and hundreds of small press publishers and editors (check out www. shawguides.com). They happen all over the U.S. and I suggest that you research them and attend. Most well organized events will offer a list of publishers who will have a tabletop display. They'll list attending editors, and advertise workshops. This gives you the opportunity to look up the people and presses attending. Read about what types of books or material they publish, how they prefer to be approached, and their general philosophy of why they got into business.

Here's what I do: I look up the presses on the internet and find out what their particular interests are, and compare that with what I'm writing. Then I check out how many reviews their books have received — a few good reviews means that they're marketing their books. Are they using wholesalers or distributors (we'll talk more about this later)? Do I recognize any of the publisher's titles? Have their books won any awards — even small awards are important. Finally, I look through their publishing history to see how many books they publish per year. If I like what I'm learning, I pick up a few of their books and read as many of their titles that I can, checking for mistakes, binding quality, subject matter, until I have a general feel about the company.

Now when I attend the conference or workshop, or the weekend book fair, I have something to talk to the publisher about. I'm familiar with what they're doing. This always helps to open the gate to a longer conversation that eventually leads to what I'm writing and how it might fit their line.

Literally every publisher I've worked with I've eventually met. Sometimes my handing a publisher a book of mine that was published by a different small press has gotten me the chance to submit my latest project for review. Occasionally, this has panned out into another book sale, and sometimes a long term relationship whether the publisher continued to publish books or not.

For example, this happened to me while attending Bookfest in Seattle. I had five copies of my first novel, "The Witness Tree" in my backpack. I was very careful who I handed them to. Impressed by a particular publisher's books, I started a conversation. The publisher and editor for Russell Dean & Company and I hit it off pretty well. We read similar books and I liked what he told me about the books he'd already published. We swapped business cards. I dropped off a copy of "The Witness Tree" and ordered several of his titles when I got home. The books were well edited and interesting, and I thought I might send in a query about my latest project.

But before I sent him the query, he contacted me — by phone. Here, he not only wanted to know what project I was working on, he also wanted to know if my previous publisher would allow him to sell "The Witness Tree" through the Russell Dean & Company catalog. Eventually, RDC published Wolf's Rite, my award-winning second novel about an advertising executive who goes through a Native American vision quest.

For another one of my novels, "The Resurrection of Billy Maynard", a chance meeting at the BookExpo America show gave me the incentive to contact the editor/publisher after returning home. That meeting helped in getting my work read, and eventually accepted for publication.

The other, often more efficient, way to find small press publishers who might be interested in your project is through directories like the "Writer's Market" or "The International Directory of Little Magazines & Small Presses". These directories can be picked up on sale the year after they come out. For small press publishers that have been around for a while, these directories maintain their relevance for several years. But, there are always those listings for presses that didn't make it through and are no longer publishing. To be sure that the smaller presses are still alive, I look online before I submit anything. Another way I test to see if they're still publishing is to send them a post card asking if they are accepting manuscripts and if so are there any time restrictions on when to send them. Some presses only read during certain months of the year. This postcard either gets a fast response, because it's easy to fill out, or it gets no response, which usually means the press has folded.

Using directories like the ones mentioned, you have the opportunity to contact many publishers at once. For poets, this is essential to getting published. Small, independent and university magazines and journals receive so many submissions and it takes the editors so long to go through all that work that it can take months and months before you hear back from them. I send up to four poems to each magazine and then rotate those poems through my list of possible publishers. If a poem is accepted, I send only those that are left until all the poems have been published. This is a great way to keep poems in circulation, and increases the potential for getting published.

This same method can work for short stories, flash fiction, and even book length projects if you've written a number of them. Over the years, I've written literally hundreds of poems, twenty or so short stories, and fifteen novels. Not everything has been published, but I keep sending the work out to publishers (often in a rewritten form). And I keep writing new material. Publishers like to know that you continue to write. That you're committed to the craft, to the art.

Although the general rule is to query first for novels, I have more than once contacted a small press publisher by phone. This is not something you want to do with most large publishing houses that have secretaries and receptionists — not to mention voicemail — who are willing and able to keep you from reaching an editor.

Small publishers operate differently. Besides having fewer employees between you and them, many are social people who enjoy being in the public. But more importantly, they enjoy what they're doing. Talking with someone who appreciates the hard work they've put into producing a book is actually a pleasure for them.

Since I often read the books they've already published before I make my call, for much of the conversation I discuss their titles to find out what the publisher/ editor liked about them to begin with. If I like the person I'm talking with and I think they might like my work, then I pitch them on my novel. Again, this may not get you a sale. It may not even get you read. But, you can make friends in the business you work in, and you get to talk about subjects you enjoy – writing and books.

When pitching to small presses, whether through a query letter and chapters or directly over the phone or at conferences and book fairs, remember that these editors are open to new authors. Although small publishers are often in it for the art, they still dream of finding the next best thing, even the next best selling author (many best selling writers started out with a small press). Your personal enthusiasm and personality do matter to these publishers because they're going to work more closely with you throughout the process than would an editor of a major publisher. Small press publishers live and die by their authors and their authors' help in producing a beautiful product.

And finally, for most small press publishers, it's about your book's content. It's great if you're a high profile professional who lectures around the country, but it's not necessary. You could be a lone researcher, a scholar of a certain subject, and if you write a good book you can get published.

Finding a publisher is only the beginning in a long

and important relationship. So, after the research, the mailings, and the acceptance, there are other steps to take and things to learn. For instance, how do you work with the editor to make your book the best it can be?

Chapter 5: The Editing Process

The pros and cons of the editing process can often be summed up in a single idea. One that I've mentioned before but has to be said again. The small press editor may be the only editor (or person) who looks over your work. I'm talking about small presses, as well as micro presses, that are owned and operated by either a single person or a handful of people — usually volunteers. That's how the majority of small presses work. The only other possibility is that the press outsources their editing. Otherwise you are at the mercy of the person who is busiest in the company, because the editor is also the publisher, the secretary, and the marketing director. His or her time and focus are limited.

Think of the author whose book they just published and who wants to discuss marketing. The editor may have moved onto his or her next project, yours, but there are still plenty of creative and business aspects to the job that need to get done. Plus, if the small press editor has a regular job, a family, and friends, then focus can become an even bigger problem. Some small, independent publishers incorporate their friends into the job as volunteers. They have collating parties, or book cover selection meetings. These publishers have learned how to make it fun for them even though running a small press is a tremendous amount of work.

I once worked with a friend for a year or two and we only produced one novel, The Waking Rooms by Richard Downing. It was a great book and a fun project. But he and I both had full time jobs and families. Eventually, my friend moved to Florida, I got bogged down at work, and our second project never got completed. We sold remaining copies back to Richard. Our unpublished author was forced to find a new publisher.

Hopefully you have talked with the editor and have an idea which job in the company gets the most attention. Small press publishers get into the business because they love books, so much of the time they'll spend more time on editing than any other function of the company. This works in your favor because at the end of it all, you will most likely have a good product to sell. And that's a great first step. You won't be embarrassed to hand the book over to another publisher or agent.

But even this step takes work on your part to make sure that the editing enhances the book. Just because a person has the funds and passion to publish doesn't always mean they're good at it. This doesn't mean that the person you're working with is a good editor either. Perhaps they just love books. Small publishers can be mechanics, chemical engineers, or English teachers. It's always good to find out their background to learn how well they'll perform each of the jobs they do — and again, read their books.

I suggest you have your book reviewed by book lovers and editors alike long before you send it out for publication. This assures you that most of the mistakes have been caught. I've talked about hiring proofreaders even after the book has been edited, which is always a good idea.

Small publishers tend to want to work with you, the author, to strengthen the manuscript based on your combined vision for the end product. This means that they'll opt for your take on the book. If they make a suggestion that you don't agree with, they'll often let the work stand. Because their goal is to publish something original, you get the benefit of the doubt. Many authors long for this kind of control of their work. I've heard a lot of authors say that their editor has made their book better, no doubt, but I've also heard the opposite. The small press editor/publisher puts a lot of the decision power into your hands. That can be good and bad depending on how flexible you are, but for most authors you can't beat that kind of relationship with an editor.

The good thing about working with a single person from the press is that in most cases the project will go much faster and smoother. Small publishers can get a book through the system in a few months. Larger publishers can take from 18 to 24 months. This speed to press has to do with several things, the most important being the number of titles the press publishes per year. If they're trying to get four or five projects completed then they've got to get through your project quickly. If they only publish one book per year, which is the case with literally hundreds of small presses, then they have all year to work on it.

Another concern for small publishers is how many copies of the previous book sold. Chances are the book, or books, that were published before yours (whether your title or someone else's) will be paying for the publication of your title. This is just one more reason why you might want to buy a few small press titles before you submit to a house. That's how you support the publisher. If authors don't support small publishers, they'll go away, which will only make it more difficult to get published.

What I've done for years is purposely buy small press titles that offer a synopsis that reads like something I might have written. Not only do I get to know the publisher's likes and dislikes through this type of research, I support those same publishers, which in turn increases the chances of them staying alive and possibly reading one of my manuscripts. Such books are often some of the best books I've read. They are fresh and different and truly enjoyable.

Chapter 6: The Production Process

Production is one subject that has suddenly gained more focus. There are many ways to produce a book. A typed manuscript (printout) is "produced" to a certain effect. An e-book first has to be formatted and laid out, which can also be considered being "produced". But, for this chapter, I want to focus more on a physical book, one with a cover and printed pages, whether hardback or paperback.

To me, physical production is important, especially now, when there are new methods of producing a book that are easier and cheaper. I'd like to think that making things easier or cheaper is a good idea, but when it comes to creative endeavors, that may not be the case. The truth is that I can write and publish a book in a physical format so easily and inexpensively now that thousands of people who are not very good at the actual craft of writing are getting published in book form.

This is primarily becaue of the availability of Print On Demand (POD) technology, which has made it easy for publishing companies to crop up all over the world that produce actual printed books that have never been passed by an editor of any kind. These books go from typed page to printed book. This puts a stigma on the work of anyone who publishes in this manner, regardless of whether the writing is any good or not. For example, if I have only a few thousand dollars to work with I can start my own publishing company – remember, there are thousands of them out there – and produce physical books. This can be done without editing or proofreading. And it's done every day.

When it becomes too easy to produce a title, the quality can slip pretty fast. But, at the same time, experimental works can now find an outlet they may not have found. And these works are important to the growth of the industry and to creativity as a whole.

So, it's important to recognize that if you are publishing with a press that provides POD titles that there are people who don't trust the quality of the writing. If you didn't get the editing work done up front, on your own, then there could easily be too many mistakes to count. At the same time, if the press is publishing experimental works similar to something you're doing, then the readers of those types of books will find out and there'll be a growing audience for your book also.

This wary attitude toward inexpensive formats is not always the case. In fact, thanks to large publishers like TOR, e-books are becoming a more viable and trusted product. In a similar manner, recognized brands like McGraw Hill are changing the way people look at POD titles. Publishers with established lines that go through continual revisions, such as textbooks, offer POD titles to keep the cost of printing down. Other publishers, small and large, use POD technology to keep a book available in print format. Some large publishers are taking on niche titles now that there is less of a concern over having low sales volumes. You can sell fewer copies each year and still make a profit off of that title.

Now let's turn to production quality. Readers of printed books, especially, have learned to expect a high standard in production quality. You don't want your book to disappoint them. If you've done your homework and read a few of the books published by a prospective small press, you'll also have noticed the quality of the physical production. Whether produced on a printing press or through a POD service, quality is noticeable. Some glues don't last long before they lose their adhesion and begin to crack or break down. The pages of a paperback may start to fall out even before you've finished reading the book. The cover stock can be so thin that the dry ink curls it back so that the cover looks as though it's already been read a few hundred times. Covers can also be produced in black and white rather than color. Unless done professionally, these titles don't look as good as they might, and may come with a sense that the editing was lacking as well. You shouldn't judge a book by its cover, but many of us do. After all, it's your first introduction to the book, your first impression of the publishing company.

For hardbacks, not only does the glue have to hold but the stitching that connects the pages and the cover has to be sewn correctly so that the cover doesn't fall off two weeks after you get the book home. Also, hardback books can be assembled by attaching the color cover from the paperback version directly to the hard cardboard cover of the book. This method is called a library cover because many libraries need a more durable way to keep the book looking good, and slipcovers are too easily lost or damaged. Some readers want slipcovers on their books because that denotes a professional job to them.

Cover art is part of the production cycle even though the editorial and/or marketing departments may have input. I've talked about this before, so I'll only say briefly that you have to make sure that your cover not only suits your book, but that it looks as though it has been professionally designed. Get an artist friend involved; hire a graphic artist if you have to. Some publishers have learned that the right cover helps to sell the book and have already done the legwork in getting professional help. Other small presses aren't as concerned about the cover. You have to be.

I'm putting quantity — press run — down as a production issue because, for print publishers, once the book is finished being printed it probably won't go back to press unless there are huge sales. There are ways to suggest larger print runs from a publisher that I'll discuss in the chapter on negotiation, but suffice it to say that a discussion about the quantity of books printed is important to you. The more books they print, the lower the cost per book, which means that they'll make more money, but only if the book sells enough copies. Before you discuss quantity with your publisher, you have to think long and hard about how many copies you can sell on your own. Then discuss how many copies the publisher typically sells of each book. This combination can help you and your publisher to understand what a reasonable count should be. More on this later.

To end the discussion on quantity, I have to go back to the discussion from the beginning of this chapter. Many small presses are offering their books through several methods: e-books, POD, and short run printings. This is a good way for them to use the technology to keep a book in print, or to try a book out before going to a large print run.

Again, read the books that a publisher puts out and examine the physical production: does the cover curl because it's not of a heavy enough weight, do pages fall out if you crack the binding to read it, and are the internal pages heavy enough not to tear while turning them?

Chapter 7: Distribution Channels

Small, independent publishers distribute their books in a variety of ways. Narrow niche publishers have often collected a direct mail list over the years for almost everyone interested in their subject. They may not need to go through bookstores, grocery stores, or museum shops. In fact, such places wouldn't sell their books very well anyway. This is especially true for publishers of books that cover the hard sciences and technical information. There're a limited number of sales a publisher can expect when publishing books that explain the formulas for plastic materials, for instance. Or, if you're looking for a specific engineering title on how to apply a certain type of motor to an application, your locally owned and operated bookstore won't have it on the shelf. But the publisher of that book may have sold a thousand copies to engineers on his or her list, or through magazines that cater to those readers.

Poetry magazine publishers who branch into publishing chapbooks or books often sell to their own lists. Their sales may be only a few hundred copies, but it's a steady sell and enough for them to print the next book and the next one. Similarly, the publisher of a line of books on a particular Indian tribe will most likely know its audience. The publisher will be able to reach that audience directly, as well as through a limited number of specialty stores, whether those dealing with Native American books or those associated with museums that highlight items from the particular tribe.

Before I go on, let's quickly discuss online bookstores as a distribution method. There is no doubt that almost every publisher in the business today, including the ones I mention, are listing their books online so that they might get just one more sale from the book they're selling. The best use of an online bookstore is when the reader knows what they're looking for. Many users go to online bookstores as a "destination". They do very little browsing. Online bookstores are most often used by people who know the title or author of the book they want to read. The point, really, is that you can't consider an online bookstore as a reliable distribution network. They are, in fact, a bookstore, and even though they warehouse some books, most are acquired through a wholesaler (which

I'll explain in a moment).

How do small presses reach bookstores in order to sell their titles? Many of them don't, and that's an issue you need to take up with your publisher. If you believe that distribution through bricks-and-mortar bookstores is important, there are several ways a small press can do that.

Many small publishers produce their own catalog and mail it to bookstores. This is a method that may get your books into some independent bookstores, but seldom works to get books into the chain bookstores. Even the independents must go through extra paperwork every time they work with a small press catalog. And extra paperwork means extra hours at work. The books the small press sells have to fit the independent's theme – if they have one – in order for them to go through the trouble. For example, an independent bookstore located in a small coastal town may purchase a series of nautical titles from several different small presses. If the books are a popular item, they'll be glad to do the paperwork. This works particularly well for niche publishers. Another example might be an independent that sells a large number of sports books. They'll be willing to put in the extra work necessary to acquire a line of, let's say, baseball books, from a small press.

A lot of independent bookstores, particularly, will purchase from small publishers who are owned and operated locally. These stores are community stores. They know the people in the area and they will work together to help those local publishers and authors. I've seen a local author section in many small town stores in particular. Even self-published titles can find their way into these stores.

Even the chain bookstores often provide a way to incorporate books produced by local authors and presses. The managers of chains have a small portion of their budget that allows them to participate in the community by supporting the local businesses and authors. Some are more difficult to get into than others, but it's always worth trying.

In general, there are two primary methods, though, to sell into bookstores: through the use of either wholesalers or distributors. Wholesalers can be viewed as service providers to bookstores. What they do is get the books from a warehouse to the bookstore for the lowest cost. All the bookstore has to do is order them. So, a small press has to create the demand for the book, then a bookstore will order it through the wholesaler. The wholesaler does not have sales people who create demand for the books in the first place. They are, basically, a warehousing, shipping, and handling outfit.

Small publishers who use wholesalers will produce a catalog, but instead of forcing the bookstore to order directly from them, they'll list prominently the names of the wholesalers who carry their titles. This makes it easy for the bookstore. They can order through one source. The paperwork is simpler, which means that they're more likely to order your titles if they see a demand from their audience. The small press still has to create the demand.

Distributors represent the interests of book publishers. Instead of a small press hiring a sales team and marketing staff, and operating its own storage, shipping, and returns warehouse, it can outsource these activities to a book distributor. This doesn't mean that a small press can sit back and let the distributor do all the work. Let's face it, a distributor will have thousands of books it's trying to get off its shelves. The small press you're publishing with may have only ten books among those thousands.

Once again, the press does have to create demand. What's good about a distributor is that once demand is created, and books from the small press begin to sell, the distributor will help those books along by talking about them to bookstores. So if you and your small press partner can create enough sales, the distributor becomes more and more interested in helping get those books into more and more stores. Generally speaking, a small, independent press can use all the help they can get, and using a distributor is typically the best method to use at first.

I've mentioned the need for a small press to create demand, and one of the best ways for them to do that is through marketing – our next subject.

Chapter 8: Marketing

The pros and cons of marketing for small presses revolve around money and time. Even large publishers require that beginning authors do a lot of their own marketing, but small publishers depend on it. Nonetheless, small presses do provide opportunities to new authors, which we will get to in a moment.

A small publisher has a limited budget for any one internal operation. Its main aim is to produce books, so its marketing department (if it has one) will most likely be lacking somewhat. As with distribution, marketing works best when the publisher is in a particular niche. Whether such publishers produce books of non-fiction or fiction, they know where their readers are and can reach those readers using a number of direct methods.

Marketing to a niche may include targeted internet

sites, attending fairs and events, a reading or lecture series, displays at specialty shops, or even a direct mail list of known readers and collectors. It doesn't matter whether the niche is football or occult romance, the small publisher may have spent years developing the market and therefore has a direct knowledge associated with the whereabouts of those readers.

But even if the small press has a developed list of markets, it will still need your help in reaching them. Money and time being the issues, as an author you might consider setting aside a budget that can be used to help your small press publisher get to its readers. The publisher will most likely be able to tell you what it costs for certain types of standard marketing that they do. Adding to their dollars is a good way to keep their attention on your project.

Time is an equally important item on their agenda. As an author, you want as much of your publisher's time as you can get. Now that the book is available, and you know that they're onto their next project, it's especially important that you keep them at least partially focused on marketing your book. If they are going to street fairs or local events and you are within easy traveling distance, help them set up, suggest that you sign books or do a reading, or a lecture. Help them prepare media kits to send to interested reviewers. Create your own postcards or bookmarks that they may want to put inside other titles they have to sell. All it has to do is have a cover shot, a short blurb explaining what the book is about, and where to buy the book.

There are numerous books available concerned with low-cost marketing ideas, and it is worth the time and effort to read them. Small publishers that focus on editing or on book production will not always have as clear a grasp on marketing as you might have. Help them out by making suggestions, adding to their budget, and spending time stuffing envelopes, making follow-up calls, or helping out at events.

There is at least one group of people it is guaranteed they will not have on their list of buyers, and that is your personal contact list. If you don't have one, create a list of friends, neighbors, relatives, and work mates. This list alone can add to the sales of your book. And, if your book is similar to other titles the small press has published, they'll be able to direct market their next title to your list in the future. They'll also add your book to the lists that other authors may have passed along. Growing an email, or address list is often one of the easiest and most effective method used to create a growing audience for a small publisher.

So, the good news about working with a small press is that if they've been around for a while, there's a chance that they have an established reader base that can only grow. If they understand their niche well, and have worked hard at getting their books into the hands of readers they may even have market share of the books they're selling.

The cons, as with other sections of this book, include the lack of time and money to do all the things they'd like to do. Sometimes, it involves the lack of professional help, too. This means that anything an author can provide will be appreciated.

I suggest that you to take the time to plan your marketing before you even pitch your book. Some small publishers have actually started to ask for a marketing plan before they'll consider a new author. Your book will always be the number one reason they select your work as their next project, but a well thought out marketing plan will let them know that you've thought more deeply about the need for your book and that you'll be a willing and able partner along the way.

Besides books that are filled with marketing ideas, there are a few books out now that suggest that you gain an audience – and essentially begin selling your book – before you even send out your query or proposal. The idea is that if you already have a platform (a following based on your expertise and/or your appearances) for your book, it will garner more sales, and most likely have steady sales as long as you continue to lecture, blog, and make appearances. As true as this is for both large and small publishers, creating a following is not as easy to do for fiction as it might be for non-fiction. If you have a full time job and are supporting a family, it creates a road-block in building a platform. Plus, if you're writing in a field where there is already a glut of high rollers, getting noticed may literally take years. And those are years that you are not focusing on the writing of your books. Make sure that you balance writing with marketing in a way that doesn't have you creating a great marketing but having little time to work on perfecting your manuscript.

I've purposely spent less time on marketing than on other sections of this book because there are so many great resources on how to market what you've written. Realize that marketing is an important part of selling your books these days. Gaining even the slightest knowledge in this area is beneficial. If I had to suggest just one book on marketing it would be "Guerrilla Marketing for Writers" by Jay Conrad Levinson, Rick Frishman, and Michael Larsen. But there are plenty more available, so ask your local bookstore owner.

I've hinted at the types of negotiations you are likely to be able to make with your small press publisher. The next chapter expands that conversation.

Chapter 9: What You Can and Can't Negotiate

Small publishers tend to be more negotiable about the details of deals than larger publishers. Many small, and most micro, presses don't even use a contract, especially those that publish poetry chapbooks. I've entered a lot of chapbook contests where the only thing you receive are copies of the chapbook itself. Small and micro presses often collect reading fees from contests and use it to pay for other books the press publishes.

For contests, there are typically no negotiation points because the 'prize' has already been established in the rules. Once accepted you may be able to negotiate the quantity of books published if you give up a monetary award (if there is one). In this way, you can assure that more copies will reach readers. Or, if you're inclined, you can purchase additional copies with your winnings, and in this way have additional copies as you read at your local bookstore, library, coffee shop, or bar.

Note that for publishers who do use a contract, all negotiations should be made before you sign. For book-length projects negotiations for an advance, if there is an advance at all, is very limited. Some publishers will allow you to trade your advance for additional marketing dollars, others might adjust the number of books they print. Since advances from the smaller publishers are typically very small or non-existent – that's why agents don't attempt to sell your novel to a small press – there isn't much to negotiate against. Although most offer no advance, some offer anywhere from a few hundred dollars to a few thousand dollars. If there is an advance, I suggest that you either keep the money aside and use it for meals and hotel rooms while you're promoting your book, or negotiate for a larger press run. After all, you either want to have more books available for readers or you want to reach more readers personally.

While we're on the subject of quantity, I've mentioned before that if you pre-sell your book there is a greater possibility that the publisher will be willing to print more copies. This means that a wholesaler or distributor can shelve more copies and therefore have them readily available for sale.

If you have a marketing plan and it includes going to a bookseller association show, a lecture to a room full of reviewers, or any other group that could have a positive effect on the sales of your book, it is possible to negotiate for additional free copies to be sent to these events. I suggest that you negotiate for up to a hundred or so copies up front, even if you haven't booked an event yet. This makes sure that the copies are available if you need them. These 'give-aways' are highly effective in getting your book read and into bookstores. There are literally dozens of bookseller associations across the U.S., and they are very willing to work with new authors for free signings at their local shows.

I have found that small publishers, especially those with well-defined, niche markets, are willing to negotiate on the discount you get when buying copies. I take copies of my books to every workshop or event I attend. Having additional copies around is essential in my plan to garner as many readers as possible. If I can get a greater discount when buying books from the publisher, it saves me up-front dollars that I can then put into travel or meals while I'm promoting my books.

Depending on where your publisher is located, there are often local events they attend. You can negotiate to stay with them or one of their friends in exchange for being available to help them sell their books, and yours, at the event. Equally, you can suggest that they might fly or drive to your local events to show their support for the project.

Marketing dollars and duties are also negotiable. How much will they spend on marketing, how much will you spend, and who will produce the pieces. All this can be talked about, should be talked about, up front while the deal is being made. I know I've mentioned this before, but I wholeheartedly suggest you read a few books about how to market your book. Then create a detailed plan (see appendix B) even before you begin to mail your manuscript out.

Many of the negotiations that I've requested up front in the past have to do with marketing, but that's not all to be concerned with. These next few items have to do with the overall quality of the end product. First of all, do everything you can to get the publisher to provide galleys whether in single sheets of paper or bound. Galleys offer you three things: a look at how the book visually comes across in printed form, a standard (and professional) method of reaching reviewers, and one more chance to catch mistakes before the book goes to the printer.

Negotiate for a proofreader to go through the book. Editing is one thing, but proof reading takes a whole other set of skills. A proofreader will catch the details that an editor will pass right over. Where an editor may catch point-of-view shifts or structural problems, a proofreader is trained in catching syntax errors and punctuation mistakes. If you have to pay someone outside the publishing company for proofreading services, negotiate who pays the person, and possibly who selects the person who'll do the job.

Now is the time to negotiate production quality as well. If the small press contracts with a printer already the quality of cover stock or the inside pages may be something that the publisher selected a year or more in advance in order to get the best deal for all the books he or she publishes. Sometimes you may have a chance to negotiate for paper stock, but not always. What you can negotiate on is whether the book is presented in a hardback or paperback form. Most authors don't realize that everything in the production of the book can be the same except that the cover is put on differently. In the past, I've negotiated that a limited quantity of hardbacks be produced so that I could sell them for a much higher price to a few collectors I know. The publisher was easily swayed once I had several pre-sold orders in hand. The cost of shipping a dozen or so copies to a company that will do the hardback bindings is minimal in exchange for the higher sale cost. After the books were set aside, I signed and numbered the hardbacks for sale.

Another element of production is the cover quality. I've mentioned this before. Covers do sell books. I read once that a potential new buyer has to see the cover of a book an average of eight times before they'll pick it up and examine its contents. A professionally produced cover helps to sell books in the end. Whether the small press you're working with has a graphics person on staff or uses a freelancer, I always ask whether I'm able to make suggestions, and/or get a few ideas together from other freelancers. Since I work with artists sometimes for my full-time job, I have access to professionals in the business. Not everyone has this opportunity, but most people have either met or known someone who can help out in this area. I have learned not to rely on my personal taste when a professional is available.

As a final note, I'd like to suggest that you put into your contract that you have the choice to buy all remaining copies of your book for the cost of printing them if, for any reason, the publisher should go out of business.

Small publishers are volatile businesses. They run out of money or time or interest. Having the ability to buy back copies of your book may mean the difference in it being available to readers or not. You want your book to be available. Along with this point, always make sure there is a clause in your contract, somewhere, that turns the rights to the book back to you if the press should fold. If you are uncomfortable reviewing the contract yourself, find a lawyer who has handled copyright law and consult with him or her keeping the items I mentioned here in mind.

Chapter 10: Internet and Self-Publishing

A lot of publishers are getting involved with Internet publishing these days. It's easy to create an e-book with a minimum of training. It's inexpensive when compared with traditional print publishing. And the end product can be distributed almost anywhere in the world. What's not to like? E-books, if they are to be taken seriously, must be produced through reputable publishers – small or large. To determine who you consider reputable, use the same suggestions I've discussed so far: content, cover art, editing, layout and product, and distribution.

I mentioned earlier that TOR offers a series of e-books on their site. There are many other publishers who automatically create an e-book – they have the digital files anyway – at the same time they produce printed copies of a book. For genres like science fiction, where the readers are often tech-savvy, e-books are bought, read, and produced in higher quantities than in other genres. It's hard to say just how many e-books are available because of the easy access to the technology. There's no clearinghouse keeping track of e-publishing.

Most agents and mainstream publishers consider your e-book, when published by an established press, a viable publishing credit. This also goes for online magazines that operate through universities, as well as other small presses that produce a different print version than its online version. And, e-books and online magazines are becoming more professional and more recognized every day.

When considering a publisher that will produce only an e-book of your project, consider most of the items already mentioned in this book. You want to have an editor work with you, you want a professional cover design, and you want a marketing and distribution plan that makes sense. You want to know that the books are getting reviewed and that the publisher is actually selling copies to readers.

Since e-books require no warehousing, no wholesaler, and no shipping, copies can get out faster and at a lower cost. This can affect the author because it is possible to get an actual count on sales. Where print copies can sit on a shelf, downloaded e-books are paid for at the time of the sale. Royalties can then be paid out on actual sold copies.

Although you can't carry copies to trade shows and fairs, you can carry well-designed and produced pamphlets, post cards, and bookmarks. You can perform readings. And, for companies with the best tech teams, you can sell copies using a special code that allows a person who heard you read – and bought your book at the reading – to go home and download your book.

The Internet is here to stay, and it can help you to get your book into the hands of readers if you've done all the legwork up front, including having a well written and edited book. Large publishers often publish several hundred print titles in a year and then wait to see which author/book works its way to the top of the list. The good part about Internet publishing in all its forms is that your book has the same chance as any other book to be one of those titles that climbs to the top. Without the concern over warehousing and physical distribution your e-book is just as available from a large publisher as a small one, considering that they have similar marketing opportunities.

If you've decided that Internet publishing is the way to go, I suggest that you might also consider a self-published print version if the Internet publisher isn't going to provide a POD version.

Of course, self-publishing conforms to the same discussion I've had throughout this book. If you've done your homework and produced a good book, it will sell based on the amount of marketing and distribution time that is put into it. A book salesman friend of mine once said that for small press (this includes Internet and self-published books, too) titles, "when you stop marketing them, they stop selling." This brings me back to time and money, which I've discussed a few times already.

Commercial publishers take an average of 18 to 24 months to bring a book out in print, and small presses take around 4 to 12 months (or more). Self-publishing, which can take as little as a week or two, might make sense if you're in a hurry. Of course, since you are paying for the books, you get all the profits from sales (after costs like printing, postage, your time, etc.). If your book is in a very low volume niche, and you know where and how to reach that niche, then you've already got what it takes to self-publish and reach your audience. This is especially true if you've written a book on a regional topic. Most of your sales may very well be in that same region, and there may only be so many places to sell such a book. Along this same line is the book that is merely written to pass along the details of your life to your loved ones. A book written for your own family members may not have the need for a wide distribution, but it's just as important to publish it.

Some self-publishing houses try to make the issue of control and sole ownership important, but if you pay attention to your contract, that's not such a big issue. Along with a commercial house owning a portion of movie sales, for instance, they also have a more direct line to the studios. This makes for a pretty good trade-off. And if control means that you want to skip past the experience of working with a good editor, then I suggest you rethink your decision. But, if control means that a larger publisher is trying to water down your opinions or change your technical details, then by all means take control if it's what you believe in.

As a final note, I'd like to urge everyone reading this to remember one thing: if you want your book to sell, you have to be a buyer as well. When you find books you enjoy, buy additional copies for friends, be vocal about recommending them. Mention the titles on Face-Book and MySpace and Twitter. Talk about small press titles and small press publishers will be alive and well for years to come.

Apendix A: A Few Resources

Most of us research on the Internet these days, which has made it fairly easy to find useful directories of poetry or fiction publishers, niche nonfiction publishers, or most anything else. I use the Internet all the time, but double-check my findings regularly. Below are a few print and online resources you might try out.

Here are what I believe to be the top three print directories in the business:

The International Directory of Little Magazines and Small Presses, published by Dustbooks (www.dustbooks.com).

Jeff Herman's Guide to Book Publishers, Editors, & Literary Agents, published by Sourcebooks (www.sourcebooks.com).

Writer's Market, published by F+W Media (www. fwbookstore.com/category/writing).

Here are a few Internet sites that I use regularly:

Provides lists of publishers, journals, awards, etc: http://www.poetrysociety.org/psa-links.php

Newpages offers a guide to independent publishers and University presses: http://www.newpages.com/NP-Guides/bookpubs.htm

Small Press Distribution: publishers that distribute through this network are typically active in the industry: http://www.spdbooks.org/root/index.asp

Chapbook publishers: http://www.everywritersresource.com/chapbooks.html

Provides lists of publishers accepting e-submissions: http://www.andromeda.rutgers.edu/~lcrew/pbonline. html

Provides a list of self-publishing companies: http://www.writersdigest.com/article/directory-of-self-publishing-companies/

Apendix B: Marketing Plan Example

Media Kit pieces:

Folder

Cover shot pasted to front of folder (I suggest doing at an angle on purpose)

Inside: Author photo

Short news release & Long news release

Synopsis of Book

Author Bio (short and long if necessary)

Q&A about Book for newspapers/radio to use

Q&A about Author for newspapers/radio to use

Review copy of book if appropriate

List with mag/newspaper blurbs from reviews

Several pages of complete reviews

Note about your 'book group kit' which includes:

Reader's Guide

Special book plate (signed) created for your book

only

Bookmark (can be something special that relates to the book)

CD or DVD with audio or video interview (even if home done)

Email address/phone: option to answer questions if you can't go to their meeting

Invitation to join your E-newsletter list (and get special rates on other books)

Contest entry: buy 5 copies for friends and get entered to win (you decide what they win).

Marketing Plan:

General Comments: Set the official publication date for six or more months 'after' actual book is to be printed. You can still sell books locally, get copies to reviewers, etc. You can also sell pre-publication copies.

Action: Create an Internet site
When: Prior to doing any marketing.
Materials: You can do it yourself or hire someone
Quantity: 1 site
Costs: Varied
Comments: The site should have available all the things put into the media kit, plus downloadable elements like audio, video, etc.

Action: Mail to major mags (Publishers Weekly, Library Journal, Kirkus, etc.)

When: 6 months before official publication date

Materials: Book galleys (or printed book), release, marketing plan, cover shot

Quantity: 25-50 plus

Costs: Book cost, p&H, copies ($200)

Comments: Request reviews

Action: Mail a 'pre-publication' flyer

When: 6 months before official publication date

Materials: Personal lists – e-mail and snail mail lists – and pre-pub flyer

Quantity: Your choice

Costs: Copies, E-mail (free), snail mail (minimal cost) ($100)

Comments: This is your friend and family list, your acquaintance list.

Action: Get books to local bookstores for review and to set up events

When: 1-2 months before official release date

Materials: Books and shelf-talkers

Quantity: 20-30

Costs: Books, travel, mailing, copies ($150)

Comments: Hand-carry or mail books to bookstores where you are recognized. Ask if a staff member might read the book and do a shelf talker for it. Ask to set up a signing, lecture, or other event with the store. Ask for any email list, local newspaper/radio contacts, library contacts, or book club coordinator contacts.

Action: Create and print posters
When: As needed
Materials: Computer
Quantity: As many as you need
Costs: $20 plus depending on size and color
Comments: Use posters at signings, trade shows, your party and other events.

Action: Follow-up to set up events
When: As soon as possible after delivering your books
Materials: Phone time
Quantity: As many as you can
Costs: Up to you (consider travel, meals, hotels, etc.)
Comments: Suggest that you can help with sending out a mailing. Send out your own mailing about events. Put events on your web site.

Action: Call or mail to local papers and radio/tv stations
When: Right away and around any events set up
Materials: Books, releases and time
Quantity: As many as you can
Costs: $100 plus books and time

Comments: When using a bookstore's list, always give the bookstore a plug. Specifically if you have a radio/tv or newspaper piece coming out, always ask that they plug one or two local bookstores who handle your work.

Action: Have a party.
When: On or near your official publishing date
Materials: Wine and cheese, a large room
Quantity: All your neighbors and friends (even your local paper)
Costs: Your choice
Comments: It may be best if a friend or spouse could coordinate the event so that it isn't so tough to put together, but any way you look at it, you'll sell a few books. Always push your publisher when you're doing these things by having flyers around. If the press looks good, so do you.

Action: Contact local and national Independent Bookseller Associations for lectures and signings
When: As soon after your official pub date as possible
Materials: Hundreds of books
Quantity: 100-500 books
Costs: Book cost and p&H cost
Comments: Groups like SEBA, PNBA, etc. are all around the U.S. The Independent Bookseller Associations are great places to hand out free copies of your latest book

directly into the hands of book buyers. Again, ask about events and make friends.

Action: Enter contests
When: As possible
Materials: Books and contest entry fees
Quantity: As many as you want
Costs: $200 plus
Comments: Winning contests is a great way to create more 'news' about your book. Whenever you win or are a finalist, you get to send another news release out.

Action: Get book racks into the front of the stores
When: Again, some of this is an ongoing project
Materials: Book racks can be bought with and without graphics for everything from counter-top (single book) to a standing rack for 6 books or more.
Quantity: Depends on your
Costs: $10-40 each (about)
Comments: Local Independent bookstores are best for these types of racks. Call and ask permission, and buy only what you need.

Action: Regular mailings to bookstores
When: As needed
Materials: Postcards, flyers, etc.
Quantity: 300 plus

Costs: $100 plus

Comments: Reminder mailings about your book ("Are you still stocking "My Title"?) is necessary to make sure you are stocked.

Action: Mailings to your own local list
When: Before an event
Materials: Postcards
Quantity: Up to you
Costs: $50
Comments: Always try to plant one or two people in the audience to buy a copy. Also, bring friends and relatives with you. Other customers will sit down if they see a few people already sitting.

Action: Go to trade shows, craft fairs, etc.
When: As they come up
Materials: A small table, several posters, your books
Quantity: As many as you want to attend
Costs: Dependent on type and place
Comments: Being out in the public with your books helps to sell them – even if at a later date and through a bookstore.

Action: Create a "Friend of the Writer" packet
When: Whenever you get the time
Materials: You decide: i.e. stickers, buttons ("Ask me

about…"), book marks, etc.

Quantity: As many as you need

Costs: Up to you

Comments: This is an idea I got from another writer. He asks his friends if they are willing to help him sell his books. If they say yes, he sends them a 'selling packet' that includes a bunch of stickers with the book title and cover shot, plus a button that says, "Ask me about my friend's book." He also hands out free bookmarks, refrigerator magnets, and whatever else he can think of that will help get people talking about his books.

OTHER BOOKS BY TERRY PERSUN

NOVELS

The Resurrection of Billy Maynard

A young man's discovery of himself in relation to his past.

Billy's father, William Maynard died before he was born, leaving Billy to be raised by his mother and grandparents. One summer, while working to save money for his return to college in the fall, Billy meets Jack, an ex-con. When Billy's mother, Alice, forbids him from talking with Jack, Billy begins a search to find out why, and get thrust into a past he could not have imagined.

"Billy Maynard's growth into manhood is a beautiful story, wonderfully written. The characters are clean, concise, and believable, and the writing poetic." —Amazon review.

Wolf's Rite

An arrogant ad executive reevaluates his life after going on a Native American vision quest.

"Every once in a while you read a book that not only touches you, but evokes you. This is a once in a while book. In Wolf's Rite, we are shown the good in the bad and the victory of such a finding." —Cheryl Townsend, poet and bookseller

"[Wolf's Rite is] an interesting angle on the complexities of the human spirit and one man's internal struggle! Experiencing a Vision Quest and its consequences through his [Wolf's] eyes provided a fascinating look at the multi-faceted aspect of all of our personalities." —B. Lynn Goodwin, book reviewer

Giver of Gifts

A dying man finds redemption in reconnecting with his family.

After his daughter's death in a car wreck, fifty-eight year old Jim finds himself detached from the world. He and his wife are fond but distant; he barely knows his married son. Without a sense of purpose, the news of his cancer pushes nice-guy Jim face to face with his mortality. Aware of his terminal condition, Jim embarks upon a hunting expedition with friends. Never a serious hunter, he finds himself reflecting upon his life as he wanders the woods. Shocked into the moment by a chance encounter with a magnificent trio of deer, he experiences a miraculous moment that definitively alters his outlook on his life and his family.

The Witness Tree

An artist finds that when he connects with nature he does his best work.

This book follows the growth and hardships of an artist. Lewis tries to connect with the world around him, but as he does so he loses a piece of himself. As he gets closer to nature, his art thrives, but his life fails. As he grows closer to life, his art fails and his sanity slips in and out. Ultimately, Lewis must decide where he is willing to spend his time.

"...a unique look at life, a fresh look at the struggle between art and madness, and a daring writing experiment." —Jim Barnes, Independent Publisher Magazine

POETRY

Every Leaf

A poetry collection

This collection draws from Terry's long list of previously published works. The poems from small press publications and university journals express the many emotional ups and downs of living a life with passion. As one reader has said, "This is a high accomplishment in writing: to condescend to no one, yet to hold something for us all."

Barn Tarot

A poetry collection

"Terry Persun's poems about parting — about all the losses signified by one parting — "swim down/ towards the back/ of his heart/ looking for light," and find it in the swimming itself — in the work the poems do. There is good humor here, at the edge of despair with love and work, and good writing. These poems are clean and sudden as pain, a pain that sometimes drives them into new rooms where they can surprise and energize us with their struggle and with their willingness to see clearly: "Each awakening/ from darkness comes first/ with sudden awe, then/ fright, then recollection." — Fleda Brown Jackson, winner of the 2001 Philip Levine Prize for Poetry

WWW.TERRYPERSUN.COM

Made in the USA
Charleston, SC
13 May 2011